Easy DIY Jewelry

FLIRTY

SPICY

ROMANCE

CHARMED

LEISURE ARTS, INC. • Little Rock, Arkansas

contents

18

17

28

32

1 SPICY | 4

2 ROMANCE | 26

EDITORIAL STAFF
Vice President of Editorial: Susan White Sullivan
Special Projects Director: Susan Frantz Wiles
Director of E-Commerce and Prepress Services: Mark Hawkins
Creative Art Director: Katherine Laughlin
Special Projects Designer: Patti Wallenfang
Technical Writers: Mary Sullivan Hutcheson, Frances Huddleston,
        Lisa Lancaster, and Jean Lewis
Art Category Manager: Lora Puls
Graphic Artist: Stacy Owens
Imaging Technician: Stephanie Johnson
Prepress Technician: Janie Marie Wright
Contributing Photographer: Ken West
Contributing Photo Stylists: Sondra Daniel and Christy Myers
Manager of E-Commerce: Robert Young

BUSINESS STAFF
President and Chief Executive Officer: Rick Barton
Vice President of Finance: Laticia Mull Dittrich
Director of Corporate Planning: Anne Martin
National Sales Director: Martha Adams
Information Technology Director: Brian Roden
Controller: Francis Caple
Vice President of Operations: Jim Dittrich
Retail Customer Service Manager: Stan Raynor
Vice President of Purchasing: Fred F. Pruss

56

59

79

77

3 FLIRTY | 48

4 CHARMED | 70

Library of Congress Control Number: 2013931600
ISBN-13: 978-1-4647-1174-9

CHAPTER ONE

spicy

It's easy to add exciting jewelry to your wardrobe! These spicy accessories glow with the colors of cinnamon, chili peppers, and curry. On page 90, you'll find all the information you need on jewelry making tools, supplies, and techniques. So you can get the warm look of the tropics in cool new accessories—and have fun creating each exotic piece!

CIRCLE PENDANT & SEED BEAD NECKLACES

*Pendant Necklace approx. length: 18", excluding pendant
Seed Bead Necklaces approx. length: 56" each*

You'll need:

◆ circle pendant
◆ pre-made 3-cord necklace
◆ 2 long wood beads
◆ 2 large metal-lined glass beads
◆ assorted brown, orange, yellow, and amber seed beads
◆ beading thread and beading needle
◆ chain-nose pliers
◆ jeweler's glue

Read Jewelry Making Basics, pages 90-96, before making your necklaces.

To make the Pendant Necklace:

1. Use the chain-nose pliers to carefully open and remove the cord end from one end of the necklace *(Fig. 1)*.

Fig. 1

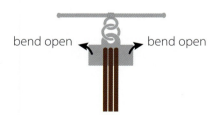

2. Thread the wood beads, glass beads, and pendant on the cords. Replace the cord end.

To make each Seed Bead Necklace:

1. With a bead stop on one end *(Fig. 2)*, thread the seed beads on a 68" beading thread length until the beaded section is 56" long.

Fig. 2

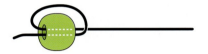

2. Remove the bead stop. Tie the thread with a surgeon's knot *(Fig. 3)* and apply a drop of glue to the knot. Once dry, trim the thread ends.

Fig. 3

3. Make as many necklaces as desired.

LINKED CHAIN BRACELET

You'll need:
- ◆ brown linked beads chain
- ◆ silver charms (we used 11)
- ◆ interchangeable charms (we used 2)
- ◆ assorted small yellow, green, and brown glass beads
- ◆ silver toggle clasp
- ◆ small and large silver jump rings
- ◆ silver eye pins
- ◆ chain-nose pliers, round-nose pliers, and wire cutters

Read Jewelry Making Basics, pages 90-96, before making your bracelet.

To make the bracelet:
1. Cut 5 lengths of chain the desired bracelet length, minus the length of the clasp.
2. To make the beaded connector, thread 1-2 beads on an eye pin. Make a loop *(page 95)* at the wire end *(**Photo 1**)*. Make 11 connectors.

Photo 1

3. Attach a silver charm to each connector with a small jump ring *(page 95)*.
4. Attach the dangles, connectors, and interchangeable charms to the chains.
5. Attach 1 end of each chain to a large jump ring. Attach the remaining ends to another large jump ring.
6. Attach the clasp to the bracelet.

TRI-COLOR NECKLACE

Approx. length: 38"

You'll need:

◆ assorted large, medium, and small red, yellow, and brown beads (we used 21)
◆ red, yellow, and brown large seed beads
◆ assorted copper spacer beads (we used 6)
◆ silver bead caps (use 2 for each desired bead)
◆ gold hook and eye clasp
◆ gold nylon-coated beading wire
◆ gold crimp beads and crimp tool
◆ chain-nose pliers and wire cutters
◆ spring bead stops

Read Jewelry Making Basics, pages 90-96, before making your necklace.

To make the necklace:

1. Leaving a 2" tail, thread three 45" wire lengths through a crimp bead and secure *(page 96)*. Trim 1 wire tail close to the crimp bead *(Fig. 1)*.

Fig. 1

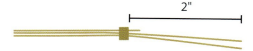

2. Attach the remaining two wires to one end of the clasp with a crimp bead. Trim the wires close to the crimp bead *(Fig. 2)*.

Fig. 2

3. Thread seed beads on each wire until the beaded section is 13$\frac{1}{2}$" long. Temporarily secure each beaded wire with a spring bead stop.
4. Holding the three wires together as one, thread the assorted beads, bead caps, and spacer beads on the wire until the beaded section is 10$\frac{1}{2}$" long.
5. Repeat Step 3 to add seed beads to the wires for the remaining side of the necklace.
6. Referring to **Fig. 1**, thread the 3 wires through a crimp bead and secure. Trim 1 wire close to the crimp bead.
7. Repeat Step 2 to attach the remaining clasp end.

BEAD & DANGLE BRACELETS

You'll need:
- assorted large, medium, and small beads and spacers (we used about 20-35 beads/spacers per bracelet)
- assorted large and medium metal beads and spacers for bead dangles
- antique copper jump rings
- antique copper head pins (for bead dangles only)
- stretch cord
- chain-nose pliers, round-nose pliers, and wire cutters (for bead dangles only)
- jeweler's glue
- flexible wire beading needle (optional)

Read Jewelry Making Basics, pages 90-96, before making your bracelets.

To make each bracelet:
1. With a bead stop at one end *(Fig. 1)*, thread assorted beads and spacers on a 12" length of cord.

Fig. 1

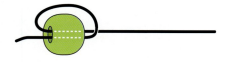

2. Check the bracelet size, adding or removing beads and spacers until the bracelet is the right length. Remove the bead stop. Tie the cord with a surgeon's knot *(Fig. 2)* and apply a drop of glue to the knot. Once dry, trim the cord ends.

Fig. 2

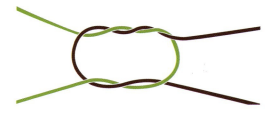

3. For the dangle bracelet, make bead dangles *(page 95)* using metal beads, spacers, and head pins. Use jump rings *(page 95)* to attach the dangles to the bracelet.

FLOWER PENDANT NECKLACE

Approx. length: 19", excluding pendant

You'll need:
◆ flower pendant
◆ 18" length each of silver, gold, and antique copper chains
◆ silver pinch bail
◆ large silver jump rings
◆ silver toggle clasp
◆ chain-nose pliers and wire cutters

Read Jewelry Making Basics, pages 90-96, before making your necklace.

To make the necklace:
1. Attach the bail to the pendant *(Fig. 1)*. Slide the pendant on all three chains.

Fig. 1

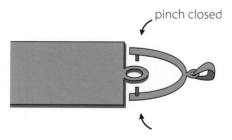

pinch closed

2. Attach 1 end of each chain to a jump ring *(page 95)*. Attach the remaining ends to another jump ring.
3. Attach the jump rings to the clasp.

STRETCHY BRACELETS

You'll need:
- ◆ assorted red and gold seed beads
- ◆ flat metal charms with attached jump rings
- ◆ ribbon
- ◆ stretch cord
- ◆ jeweler's glue
- ◆ flexible wire beading needle (optional)

Read Jewelry Making Basics, pages 90-96, before making your bracelets.

To make each bracelet:
1. With a bead stop at one end *(Fig. 1)*, thread beads (and charms) on a 12" length of cord.

Fig. 1

2. Check the bracelet size, adding or removing beads until the bracelet is the right length. Remove the bead stop. Tie the cord with a surgeon's knot *(Fig. 2)* and apply a drop of glue to the knot. Once dry, trim the cord ends.

Fig. 2

3. Make 2 bracelets with beads only and 3 bracelets with beads and charms. Tie the bracelets together with a ribbon bow.

OWL NECKLACE

Approx. length: 32", excluding pendant

You'll need:

◆ owl pendant
◆ 50" length of orange suede cord
◆ 38" length of thin jute cord
◆ 38" length of antique copper chain
◆ gold extra-large jump ring
◆ chain-nose pliers and wire cutters
◆ jeweler's glue

Read Jewelry Making Basics, pages 90-96, before making your necklace.

To make the necklace:

1. Set aside a 12" length of the suede cord.
2. Holding all 3 lengths together, thread the jump ring on the suede cord, jute cord, and chain. Centering the jump ring, fold the cords and chain in half.
3. Form a loop with the 12" suede cord length. Wrap the suede around the folded cords and chain 5-6 times. Bring the end through the loop *(Fig. 1)*. Pull firmly on the opposite end of the cord until the loop disappears.

4. Place a drop of glue on the top and bottom cord ends. When the glue is dry, trim the cord ends *(Fig. 2)*.

Fig. 2

5. Knot the chain and both cord ends together.
6. Attach the pendant to the jump ring *(page 95)*.

Fig. 1

DANGLE EARRINGS

You'll need:

◆ 12 assorted large, medium, and small beads and spacers (in pairs)
◆ 4 silver bead caps
◆ 2 silver head pins
◆ 2 silver ear wires
◆ chain-nose pliers, round-nose pliers, and wire cutters

Read Jewelry Making Basics, pages 90-96, before making your earrings.

For each earring:

1. Make a bead dangle *(page 95)* with the beads, spacers, bead caps, and a head pin.
2. Attach the dangle *(page 95)* to the ear wire.

LINKED CHAIN EARRINGS

You'll need:
- ◆ amber linked beads chain
- ◆ 2 small bronze crystal beads
- ◆ 2 large flat metal beads
- ◆ 2 metal spacer beads
- ◆ 2 medium red flat beads
- ◆ 2 antique copper eye pins
- ◆ 2 antique copper ear wires
- ◆ chain-nose pliers, round-nose pliers, and wire cutters

Read Jewelry Making Basics, pages 90-96, before making your earrings.

For each earring:

1. To make the beaded connector, thread beads and a spacer on an eye pin. Make a loop *(page 95)* at the wire end **(Photo 1)**.

Photo 1

2. Attach the beaded connector to the ear wire *(page 95)*.
3. Fold two 4¹/₂" chain lengths in half and attach to the connector **(Fig. 1)**.

Fig. 1

CHUNKY & CHARMING BRACELETS

For the Chunky Bracelet, you'll need:
- large cream beads (we used 5)
- medium red flat beads (we used 8)
- assorted metal beads and spacers
- antique copper toggle clasp
- antique copper nylon-coated beading wire
- antique copper crimp beads and crimp tool
- wire cutters

For the Charming Bracelets, you'll need:
- large wood stick beads (we used 21)
- medium wood round beads (we used 15)
- small silver round beads (we used 15)
- flat disc charms with attached jump rings (we used 8)
- stretch cord
- jeweler's glue
- flexible wire beading needle (optional)

Read Jewelry Making Basics, pages 90-96, before making your bracelets.

To make the Chunky Bracelet:
1. Use a crimp bead *(page 96)* to attach one end of the clasp to a 14" wire length.
2. Thread the beads and spacers on the wire. Check the bracelet size, adding or removing beads until the bracelet is the right length.
3. Use a crimp bead to attach the remaining end of the clasp to the bracelet.

To make each Charming Bracelet:
1. With a bead stop at one end *(Fig. 1)*, thread beads (and charms) on a 12" length of cord.

Fig. 1

2. Check the bracelet size, adding or removing beads until the bracelet is the right length. Remove the stop bead. Tie the cord with a surgeon's knot *(Fig. 2)* and apply a drop of glue to the knot. Once dry, trim the cord ends.

Fig. 2

PEACOCK PENDANT NECKLACE

Approx. length: 24", excluding pendant

You'll need:
- peacock pendant with attached bail
- small silver beads (we used 130)
- small brown wood beads (we used 115)
- small green glass beads (we used 40)
- silver lobster clasp
- large silver jump rings
- silver nylon-coated beading wire
- silver crimp beads and crimp tool
- chain-nose pliers and wire cutters

Read Jewelry Making Basics, pages 90-96, before making your necklace.

To make the necklace:
1. Use a crimp bead *(page 96)* to attach a jump ring to a 28" wire length. Thread the brown and silver beads on the wire until the beaded section is 23" long. Use a crimp bead to attach another jump ring.
2. Repeat Step 1 using the green and silver beads, adding the pendant at the center.
3. Attach the clasp to the necklace *(page 95)*.

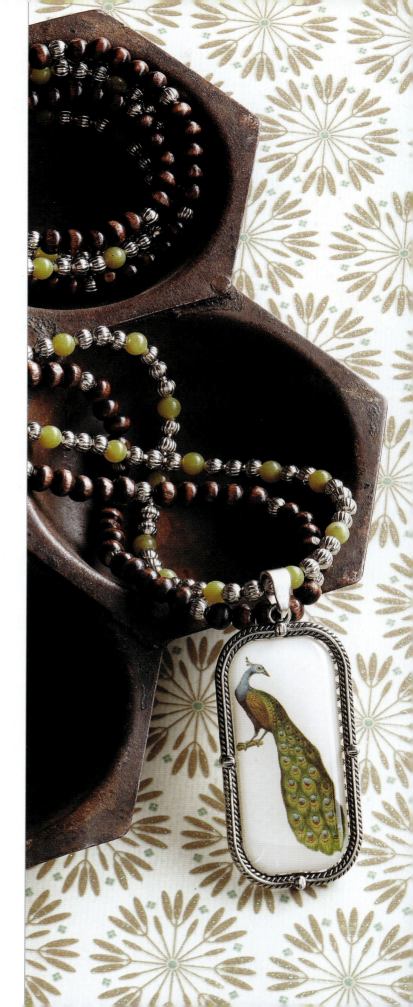

CROSS PENDANT & CHAIN NECKLACES

Pendant Necklace approx. length: 16", excluding pendant
Chain Necklace approx. length: 52"

Read Jewelry Making Basics, pages 90-96, before making your necklaces.

You'll need:
◆ cross pendant
◆ antique copper chain
◆ antique copper small jump ring
◆ antique copper extra-large oval jump ring
◆ antique copper lobster clasp
◆ chain-nose pliers and wire cutters

To make the necklaces:
1. For the pendant necklace, use the small jump ring to attach the clasp to a 15" chain length *(page 95)*. Slide the pendant on the chain.
2. For the chain necklace, use the oval jump ring to join the ends of a 52" chain length.

LEAF NECKLACE

Approx. length: 14", excluding pendant

You'll need:
◆ glass leaf pendant
◆ small brown glass beads
  (we used 95)
◆ small amber glass beads
  (we used 80)
◆ small gold glass beads
  (we used 42)
◆ gold and brown seed beads
◆ large gold jump rings
◆ gold hook and eye clasp
◆ gold nylon-coated beading wire
◆ gold crimp beads and crimp tool
◆ beading thread and beading needle
◆ chain-nose pliers and wire cutters
◆ jeweler's glue

Read Jewelry Making Basics, pages 90-96, before making your necklace.

To make the necklace:
1. Attach a jump ring *(page 95)* to the clasp eye.
2. Use a crimp bead *(page 96)* to attach the clasp eye jump ring to a 20" wire length. Thread brown beads on the wire until the beaded section is 14" long. Use a crimp bead to attach the clasp hook to the wire.
3. Repeat Step 2 using amber beads.
4. Repeat Step 2 using gold and remaining brown beads.

5. To make the beaded pendant bail, place a bead stop *(Fig. 1)* on the beading thread. Thread the seed beads on the thread until the beaded section is 4" long. Remove the bead stop. Tie the thread with a surgeon's knot *(Fig. 2)*, forming a ring. Apply a drop of glue to the knot. Once dry, trim the thread ends.

Fig. 1

Fig. 2

6. Double the beaded bail. Attach the pendant to the bail with a jump ring. Thread the pendant on the necklace.

BRACELET TRIO

You'll need:
◆ assorted beads and spacers (be sure to get a few large beads for the dangles)
◆ antique copper jump rings
◆ antique copper head pins
◆ stretch cord
◆ chain-nose pliers, round-nose pliers, and wire cutters
◆ jeweler's glue
◆ flexible wire beading needle (optional)

Read Jewelry Making Basics, pages 90-96, before making your bracelets.

To make each bracelet:
1. With a bead stop at one end *(Fig. 1)*, thread assorted beads and spacers on a 12" length of cord.

Fig. 1

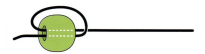

2. Check the bracelet size, adding or removing beads and spacers until the bracelet is the right length. Remove the bead stop. Tie the cord with a surgeon's knot *(Fig. 2)* and apply a drop of glue to the knot. Once dry, trim the cord ends.

Fig. 2

3. For the dangle bracelet, make 3 bead dangles *(page 95)* using the beads, spacers, and head pins.
4. Use a jump ring *(page 95)* to join 2 dangles.
5. Use jump rings to attach the dangles to the bracelet.

CHANDELIER EARRINGS

You'll need:
- ◆ 2 antique gold filigree circles with loops
- ◆ 40 assorted medium and small beads (in pairs)
- ◆ 4 flat metal charms with jump rings
- ◆ 2 gold ear wires with attached pinch bails
- ◆ 4 gold eye pins
- ◆ 6 gold head pins
- ◆ 10 gold jump rings
- ◆ chain-nose pliers, round-nose pliers, and wire cutters

Read Jewelry Making Basics, pages 90-96, before making your earrings.

For each earring:
1. Make 1 long and 2 short bead dangles *(page 95)* with assorted beads and head pins.
2. To make the beaded connector, thread beads on an eye pin. Make a loop at the wire end **(Photo 1)**. Make 2 connectors and attach a charm to each one *(page 95)*.

Photo 1

3. Attach the dangles and connectors to the circle with jump rings.
4. Attach the circle to the ear wire pinch bail **(Fig. 1)**.

Fig. 1

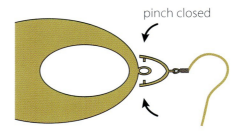

pinch closed

CHAPTER TWO

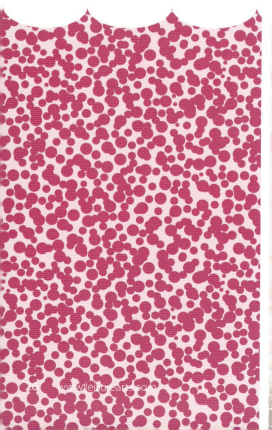

romance

Fall in love with these necklaces, earrings, and bracelets! You'll
adore how easy they are to create! You'll learn all the basics on
the jewelry making supplies, tools, and techniques you need to
make these alluring designs. In almost no time, you'll be wearing
exciting new accessories for all of life's special occasions.

CROSS NECKLACE

You'll need:
- ◆ pre-made cord/ribbon necklace
- ◆ 2 large metal-lined glass beads
- ◆ 4 jeweled pink and crystal spacer beads
- ◆ cross pendant with attached bail and faux pearl dangles

To make the necklace:
Thread the beads, spacers, and pendant on the necklace.

TIP: If the necklace clasp is a bit too wide to fit through the beads, use chain-nose pliers to gently open the clasp. Thread the beads on the necklace and replace the clasp.

HOOP EARRINGS

You'll need:
- ◆ 2 large pink metal-lined glass beads
- ◆ 4 pink jeweled spacer beads
- ◆ 2 silver hoop earrings

For each earring:
Thread the beads and spacers on the earring.

TIP: Just about everyone has a pair of hoop earrings in her jewelry box. This is a great way to accessorize them.

LOCKET & CHARM STRETCHY BRACELETS

For each bracelet, you'll need:
◆ assorted medium beads (we used about 15-18 beads per bracelet)
◆ silver locket or charm
◆ silver jump rings
◆ stretch cord
◆ jeweler's glue
◆ chain nose pliers
◆ flexible wire beading needle (optional)

For the Locket bracelet, you'll also need:
◆ silver bead caps (2 for each bead)

Read Jewelry Making Basics, pages 90-96, before making your bracelets.

To make each bracelet:
1. With a bead stop at one end *(Fig. 1)*, thread beads (and bead caps) on a 12" length of cord.

Fig. 1

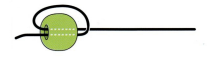

2. Check the bracelet size, adding or removing beads (and bead caps) until the bracelet is the right length. Remove the bead stop. Tie the cord with a surgeon's knot *(Fig. 2)* and apply a drop of glue to the knot. Once dry, trim the cord ends.

Fig. 2

3. Use a jump ring *(page 95)* to attach the locket or charm.

STRETCHY CUFF BRACELET

You'll need:
- medium faux pearl beads (we used 72)
- 3-hole rhinestone spacer bars (we used 8)
- stretch cord
- jeweler's glue
- flexible wire beading needle (optional)

Read Jewelry Making Basics, pages 90-96, before making your bracelet.

To make the bracelet:
1. With a bead stop *(Fig. 1)* at one end of each cord, thread beads and spacer bars on three 12" lengths of cord.

Fig. 1

2. Check the bracelet size, adding or removing beads and spacer bars until the bracelet is the right length. Remove the bead stop. Tie the cords with a surgeon's knot *(Fig. 2)* and apply a drop of glue to each knot. Once dry, trim the cord ends.

Fig. 2

FRAME NECKLACE

Approx. length: 34", excluding pendant

You'll need:
◆ faux pearl linked beads chain
◆ silver frame pendant with top and bottom loops
◆ silver cross pendant
◆ ribbon
◆ silver jump rings
◆ chain-nose pliers and wire cutters

Read Jewelry Making Basics, pages 90-96, before making your necklace.

To make the Necklace:
1. Cut a 34" length of chain. Use a jump ring *(page 95)* to attach the chain to the frame pendant.
2. Use a jump ring to attach the cross pendant to the frame pendant.
3. Tie a ribbon bow through the pendant loop.

PRETTY IN PINK NECKLACES

Pendant Necklace approx. length: 31", excluding pendant
Twisted Bead Necklace approx. length: 32"

For the Pendant Necklace, you'll need:
◆ key pendant for large metal-lined glass beads
◆ 2 large metal-lined black/white glass beads
◆ 2 pink/crystal jeweled spacer beads
◆ 1 yd narrow pink ribbon

For the Twisted Bead Necklace, you'll need:
◆ assorted pink seed beads
◆ assorted pink and white ribbons
◆ beading thread
◆ jeweler's glue

Read Jewelry Making Basics, pages 90-96, before making
your necklaces.

To make the Pendant Necklace:
1. Unscrew the top of the key pendant. Thread the beads and spacers on the pendant and replace the top.
2. Fold a 33" ribbon length in half and knot through the pendant top. Knot the ends together.

To make the Twisted Bead Necklace:
1. With a bead stop at one end **(Fig. 1)**, thread the beads on a 46" length of beading thread until the beaded section is 34".

Fig. 1

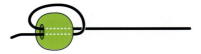

2. Remove the bead stop. Tie the thread with a surgeon's knot **(Fig. 2)** and apply a drop of glue to the knot. Once dry, trim the thread ends.

Fig. 2

3. Repeat Steps 1 and 2 to make a total of 2 beaded strands of equal length.
4. Loop the strands over one finger on each hand. Holding one hand stationary, twist the strands. Thread the ribbon through the loops where your fingers are and tie a bow, making the necklace.

SILVER CHAIN NECKLACE

Approx. length: 19", excluding pendant

You'll need:
◆ silver chain in three sizes
◆ large silver loop pendant
◆ assorted medium beads (we used 2)
◆ assorted charms (we used 5)
◆ silver lobster clasp
◆ large and small silver jump rings
◆ silver head pins
◆ chain-nose pliers, round-nose pliers, and wire cutters

Read Jewelry Making Basics, pages 90-96, before making your necklace.

To make the necklace:
1. Make 2 bead dangles *(page 95)* using head pins and beads.
2. Cut a 4" length of the smallest chain. Using a jump ring, attach a charm and the chain, folded in half, to the loop pendant *(page 95)*. Use jump rings to attach the remaining charms and bead dangles to the loop pendant, reserving a charm and a bead dangle for the top.
3. Cut an 18" length of each remaining chain. Attach the pendant to the larger chain center. Thread the remaining chain though the pendant jump ring.
4. Attach the reserved charm and bead dangle to the pendant jump ring.
5. Attach the clasp to the chain ends.

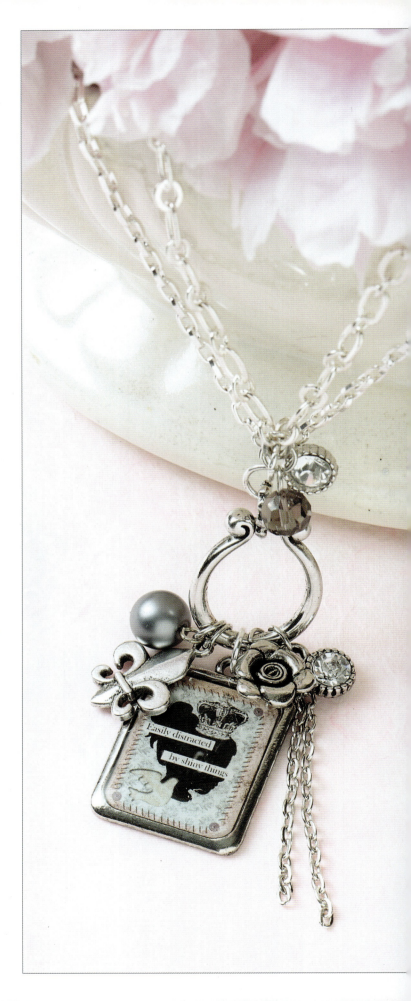

CORD & RIBBON NECKLACE

You'll need:

- ◆ pre-made cord/ribbon necklace
- ◆ 4 large metal-lined glass beads
- ◆ 4 silver large hole spacers
- ◆ silver metal spacer with attached loop
- ◆ rhinestone charm
- ◆ silver jump ring
- ◆ chain-nose pliers

Read Jewelry Making Basics, pages 90-96, before making your necklace.

To make the necklace:

1. Use the jump ring *(page 95)* to attach the charm to the metal spacer loop.
2. Thread the beads and spacers on the necklace.

TIP: *If the necklace clasp is a bit too wide to fit through the beads, use chain-nose pliers to gently open the clasp. Thread the beads on the necklace and replace the clasp.*

PEARL NECKLACE

Approx. length: 54", excluding pendant

You'll need:
◆ medium faux pearl beads (we used 180)
◆ large acrylic gemstone
◆ assorted medium and small beads and jeweled spacer beads
◆ silver head pin
◆ silver eye pin
◆ silver jump ring
◆ beading thread
◆ beading needle
◆ jeweler's glue
◆ chain-nose pliers, round-nose pliers, and wire cutters

Read Jewelry Making Basics, pages 90-96, before making your necklace.

To make necklace:
1. With a bead stop at one end *(Fig. 1)*, thread the pearls on a 66" length of thread until the beaded section is 54" long.

Fig. 1

2. Remove the bead stop. Tie the thread with a surgeon's knot *(Fig. 2)* and apply a drop of glue to the knot. Once dry, trim the thread ends.

Fig. 2

3. To make the beaded connector, thread the large gemstone on the eye pin. Make a loop *(page 95)* at the wire end *(Photo 1)*.

Photo 1

4. Make a bead dangle *(page 95)* with the remaining beads and head pin.
5. Attach the bead dangle to the connector *(page 95)*, creating the pendant.
6. Use a jump ring to attach the pendant to the necklace.

STRETCHY BRACELETS

For each bracelet, you'll need:
◆ assorted medium and small pink, faux pearl, and crystal beads (we used about 30-40 beads)
◆ stretch cord
◆ jeweler's glue
◆ flexible wire beading needle (optional)

You'll also need:
◆ ribbon

For the charm bracelet, you'll also need:
◆ assorted silver charms (we used 6)
◆ silver jump rings
◆ chain-nose pliers

Read Jewelry Making Basics, pages 90-96, before making your bracelets.

To make each bracelet:
1. With a bead stop at one end **(Fig. 1)**, thread beads on a 12" length of cord.

Fig. 1

2. Check the bracelet size, adding or removing beads until the bracelet is the right length. Remove the bead stop. Tie the cord with a surgeon's knot **(Fig. 2)** and apply a drop of glue to the knot. Once dry, trim the cord ends.

Fig. 2

3. For the charm bracelet, use jump rings *(page 95)* to attach the charms.
4. Tie the bracelets together with a ribbon bow.

DANGLE BRACELET

You'll need:

- ◆ assorted silver seed beads
- ◆ assorted medium and small faux pearl, black, and silver beads for dangle
- ◆ large clear acrylic bead for dangle
- ◆ silver head pin
- ◆ large silver jump rings
- ◆ silver nylon-coated beading wire
- ◆ silver toggle clasp
- ◆ silver crimp beads and crimp tool
- ◆ round-nose pliers and wire cutters
- ◆ spring bead stops

Read Jewelry Making Basics, pages 90-96, before making your bracelet.

To make the bracelet:

1. Use crimp beads *(page 96)* to attach three 14" wire lengths to a jump ring *(Fig. 1)*.

Fig. 1

2. Thread the seed beads on the wires, using the spring bead stop to temporarily secure the beads. Check the bracelet size, adding or removing beads until the bracelet is the right length.
3. Use crimp beads to attach the wire ends to a jump ring. Attach the clasp to the jump rings *(page 95)*.
4. Make a bead dangle *(page 95)* with the remaining beads and a head pin.
5. Use a jump ring to attach the dangle to the bracelet.

PINK & SILVER NECKLACES

Pendant Necklace approx. length: 19" excluding pendant
Pearl Necklace approx. length: 17"
Pink Necklace approx. length: 36"

For the Pendant Necklace, you'll need:
◆ pink/silver pendant with attached bail
◆ clear iridescent seed beads
◆ silver lobster clasp
◆ silver nylon-coated beading wire
◆ silver crimp beads and crimp tool
◆ wire cutters

For the Pink Pearl Necklace, you'll need:
◆ small pink faux pearls (we used 42)
◆ small pink crystal beads (we used 45)
◆ silver toggle clasp with charm
◆ silver nylon-coated beading wire
◆ silver crimp beads and crimp tool
◆ wire cutters

For the Pink Necklace, you'll need:
◆ assorted medium pink acrylic beads (we used 132)
◆ silver toggle clasp with charm
◆ silver nylon-coated beading wire
◆ silver crimp beads and crimp tool
◆ wire cutters

Read Jewelry Making Basics, pages 90-96, before making your necklaces.

To make the Pendant Necklace:
1. Use a crimp bead *(page 96)* to attach one end of the clasp to a 23" length of beading wire.
2. Thread the seed beads on the wire until the beaded section is 18". Thread the pendant on the necklace.
3. Use a crimp bead to attach the remaining clasp end to the necklace.

To make the Pink Pearl Necklace:
1. Use a crimp bead *(page 96)* to attach the loop end of the clasp to a 21" length of beading wire.
2. Beginning and ending with the crystal beads, thread the beads on the wire until the beaded section is 16". Be sure to use a few extra crystal beads near the clasp bar so you can fit the bar through the clasp loop.
3. Use a crimp bead to attach the remaining clasp end to the necklace.

To make the Pink Necklace:
1. Use a crimp bead *(page 96)* to attach the loop end of the clasp to a 40" length of beading wire.
2. Thread the beads on the wire until the beaded section is 35". Be sure to use some smaller beads near the clasp bar so you can fit the bar through the clasp loop.
3. Use a crimp bead to attach the remaining clasp end to the necklace.

SPARKLY EARRINGS

You'll need:
- ◆ tiny rhinestone chain with rhinestone chain ends
- ◆ 4 small crystal beads
- ◆ 2 medium silver/rhinestone beads
- ◆ 2 silver ear wires
- ◆ 2 silver cones
- ◆ 2 silver eye pins
- ◆ chain-nose pliers, round-nose pliers, and wire cutters

Read Jewelry Making Basics, pages 90-96, before making your earrings.

For each earring:
1. Cut three 2¹/₂" chain lengths. Attach a rhinestone chain end to the last stone on one end of each chain **(Fig. 1)**.

Fig. 1

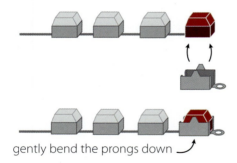

gently bend the prongs down

2. Attach the 3 chain ends to an eye pin *(page 95)*.
3. Thread the eye pin through a cone. Thread 2 crystal beads and a silver/rhinestone bead on the eye pin. Make a loop *(page 95)* at the wire end.
4. Attach the earring to the ear wire.

DANGLE EARRINGS

You'll need:
- ◆ 2 large pink acrylic beads
- ◆ 2 medium grey faux pearl beads
- ◆ 4 jeweled spacers
- ◆ 4 small crystal beads
- ◆ 2 silver head pins
- ◆ 2 large silver kidney ear wires with attached rhinestones
- ◆ chain-nose pliers, round-nose pliers, and wire cutters

Read Jewelry Making Basics, pages 90-96, before making your earrings.

For each earring:
1. Make a bead dangle *(page 95)* with the beads, spacers, and a head pin.
2. Slide the bead dangle on the ear wire.

SPARKLY NECKLACES

Pendant Necklace approx. length: 26", excluding pendant
Beaded Necklace approx. length: 45"

For Pendant Necklace, you'll need:
◆ silver pendant with attached bail
◆ rhinestone chain with rhinestone chain ends
◆ silver toggle clasp
◆ silver jump rings
◆ chain nose pliers and wire cutters

For Beaded Necklace, you'll need:
◆ assorted medium and small crystal beads
  (we used 202)
◆ beading thread
◆ beading needle
◆ jeweler's glue

Read Jewelry Making Basics, pages 90-96, before making your necklaces.

To make the Pendant Necklace:
1. Attach a rhinestone chain end to the last stone on each end of a 26" length of rhinestone chain **(Fig. 1)**.

Fig. 1

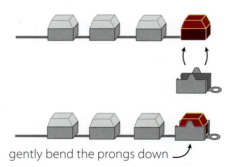

gently bend the prongs down

2. Use jump rings *(page 95)* to attach the clasp to the chain.
3. Thread the pendant on the chain.

To make the Beaded Necklace:
1. With a bead stop at one end **(Fig. 2)**, thread the beads on a 57" beading thread length until the beaded section is 45" long.

Fig. 2

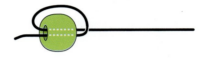

2. Remove the bead stop. Tie the thread with a surgeon's knot **(Fig. 3)** and apply a drop of glue to the knot. Once dry, trim the thread ends.

Fig. 3

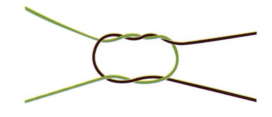

CHAPTER THREE

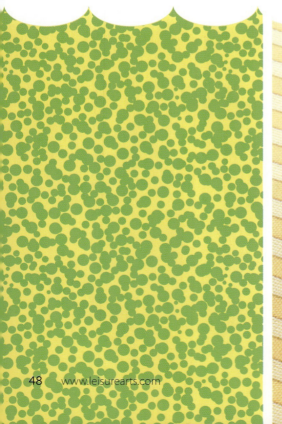

flirty

Get everyone's attention with flirty and fashionable jewelry—that you made yourself! All the easy basics on beads, findings, tools, and techniques begin on page 90. You'll be able to create these exciting designs as quick as a wink! Let their bold colors and playful themes show the world your fun side.

FEATHER EARRINGS

You'll need:
- ◆ 2 silver feather charms
- ◆ 2 small green crystal beads
- ◆ 4 small silver beads
- ◆ 2 silver ear wires
- ◆ 4 large silver jump rings
- ◆ 2 silver eye pins
- ◆ chain-nose pliers, round-nose pliers, and wire cutters

Read Jewelry Making Basics, pages 90-96, before making your earrings.

For each earring:

1. To make the beaded connector, thread the beads on an eye pin. Make a loop *(page 95)* at the wire end ***(Photo 1)***.

Photo 1

2. Use jump rings *(page 95)* to join the feather charm and ear wire to the connector.

RIBBON NECKLACE

You'll need:

◆ pre-made cord/ribbon necklace
◆ feather pendant with attached charms and tassel
◆ large bronze oval jump ring
◆ chain-nose pliers

Read Jewelry Making Basics, pages 90-96, before making your necklace.

To make the necklace:

1. Attach the jump ring *(page 95)* to the pendant.
2. Thread the pendant on the necklace.

PEACE SIGN BRACELET

You'll need:
◆ medium glass beads (we used 5)
◆ silver peace sign links (we used 5)
◆ silver toggle clasp
◆ silver eye pins
◆ small and medium silver jump rings
◆ chain-nose pliers, round-nose pliers, and wire
   cutters

Read Jewelry Making Basics, pages 90-96, before making your bracelet.

To make the bracelet:
1. To make the beaded connector, thread a bead on an eye pin. Make a loop *(page 95)* at the wire end *(Photo 1)*. We made 5 connectors.

Photo 1

2. Use the small jump rings *(page 95)* to join the beaded connectors and silver links. Check bracelet length, adding or removing connectors/links until the bracelet is the right length.
3. Attach the clasp to the bracelet with the medium jump rings.

PEACE SIGN EARRINGS

You'll need:
- ◆ 4 medium beads (in pairs)
- ◆ 2 silver peace sign links
- ◆ 2 silver ear wires
- ◆ 4 silver jump rings
- ◆ 2 silver eye pins
- ◆ 2 silver head pins
- ◆ chain-nose pliers, round-nose pliers, and wire cutters

Read Jewelry Making Basics, pages 90-96, before making your earrings.

For each earring:
1. To make the beaded connector, thread a bead on an eye pin. Make a loop *(page 95)* at the wire end *(Photo 1)*.

Photo 1

2. Make a bead dangle using a bead and head pin.
3. Use jump rings *(page 95)* to attach the dangle and connector to a link.
4. Attach the connector to an ear wire.

WHITE & GOLD BRACELET

You'll need:
- large white beads (we used 5)
- medium gold metal beads (we used 6)
- amber seed beads (we used 12)
- gold nylon-coated beading wire
- large gold jump rings
- gold toggle clasp
- gold crimp beads and crimp tool
- chain-nose pliers and wire cutters

Read Jewelry Making Basics, pages 90-96, before making your bracelet.

To make the bracelet:
1. Use a crimp bead *(page 96)* to attach a 14" wire length to a jump ring.
2. Thread the beads on the wire. Check the bracelet size, adding or removing beads until the bracelet is the right length.
3. Use a crimp bead to attach the wire end to a jump ring.
4. Attach the clasp to the bracelet *(page 95)*.

STRETCHY BRACELETS

For each bracelet, you'll need:
◆ assorted large, medium, and small beads (about 20-30 per bracelet)
◆ stretch cord
◆ jeweler's glue
◆ flexible wire beading needle (optional)

Read Jewelry Making Basics, pages 90-96, before making your bracelets.

To make each bracelet:
1. With a bead stop at one end *(Fig. 1)*, thread beads on a 12" length of cord.

Fig. 1

2. Check the bracelet size, adding or removing beads until the bracelet is the right length. Remove the bead stop. Tie the cord with a surgeon's knot *(Fig. 2)* and apply a drop of glue to the knot. Once dry, trim the cord ends.

Fig. 2

DANGLES BRACELET

You'll need:

◆ assorted large, medium, and small orange and yellow beads (we used 85)
◆ silver chain bracelet
◆ silver head pins
◆ chain-nose pliers, round-nose pliers, and wire cutters

Read Jewelry Making Basics, pages 90-96, before making your bracelet.

To make the bracelet:

1. Make bead dangles *(page 95)*, using a head pin and 1-3 beads per dangle.
2. Attach the dangles to the bracelet *(page 95)*.

PINK DANGLES NECKLACE

Approx. length: 18", excluding dangles

You'll need:

◆ assorted large, medium, and small pink and silver beads (we used 130)
◆ silver chain
◆ silver lobster clasp
◆ silver head pins
◆ silver jump rings
◆ chain-nose pliers, round-nose pliers, and wire cutters

Read Jewelry Making Basics, pages 90-96, before making your necklace.

To make the necklace:

1. Make 60 bead dangles *(page 95)* using the head pins and 1-4 beads on each dangle.
2. Attach the dangles to the center 5" of an 18" chain length *(page 95)*.
3. Use the jump rings to attach the clasp to the chain ends.

YELLOW DAISY NECKLACE

Approx. length: 40"

You'll need:
◆ 3 wood yellow daisy medallions
◆ assorted medium and small yellow and silver beads
  (we used 124)
◆ silver nylon-coated beading wire
◆ silver crimp beads and crimp tool
◆ wire cutters

Read Jewelry Making Basics, pages 90-96, before making your necklace.

To make the necklace:
1. Use a crimp bead *(page 96)* to attach a 32" wire length to a medallion *(Fig. 1)*. Thread beads on the wire until the beaded section is 28" long. Use a crimp bead to attach the remaining wire end to a second medallion.

Fig. 1

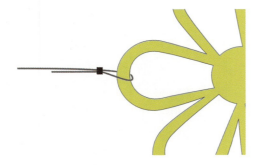

2. Use a crimp bead to attach an 8" wire length to the opposite side of the second medallion. Thread beads on the wire until the beaded section is 3" long. Use a crimp bead to attach the remaining wire end to a third medallion.
3. Use a crimp bead to attach an 8" wire length to the opposite side of the third medallion. Thread beads on the wire until the beaded section is 3" long. Use a crimp bead to attach the remaining wire end to the first medallion.

BUTTERFLY NECKLACE

Approx. length: 40", excluding pendant

You'll need:
- bronze butterfly pendant
- amber linked beads chain
- gold leather cord
- gold jump rings
- chain-nose pliers

Read Jewelry Making Basics, pages 90-96, before making your necklace.

To make the necklace:
1. Use jump rings *(page 95)* to attach the ends of a 40" chain length to the pendant.
2. Thread a 44" cord length through the pendant. Knot the ends together.

DANGLES EARRINGS

You'll need:

- 30 assorted medium and small pink and silver beads (in pairs)
- 2 silver hoop earrings
- 8 silver head pins
- 8 large silver jump rings
- chain-nose pliers, round-nose pliers, and wire cutters

Read Jewelry Making Basics, pages 90-96, before making your earrings.

For each earring:

1. Make 4 bead dangles *(page 95)* using head pins and 3-5 beads per dangle.
2. Attach a jump ring *(page 95)* to each dangle
3. Slide the dangles on a hoop earring.

TIP: *Just about everyone has a pair of hoop earrings in her jewelry box. This is a great way to accessorize them.*

BLUE DAISY NECKLACE

Approx. length: 38"

You'll need:

- 2 blue acrylic daisy beads
- 5 gold beads for daisy section
- assorted medium yellow and white beads (we used 68)
- medium clear beads (we used 66)
- large blue acrylic beads (we used 26)
- silver chain
- 2 decorative silver ovals
- large silver jump rings
- silver nylon-coated beading wire
- silver crimp beads and crimp tool
- chain-nose pliers and wire cutters

Read Jewelry Making Basics, pages 90-96, before making your necklace.

To make the necklace:

1. For the daisy strand, attach a jump ring *(page 95)* to a silver oval. Use a crimp bead *(page 96)* to attach a 10" wire length to the jump ring. Thread the gold beads and daisy beads on the wire.

2. Use a crimp bead to attach the wire end to a jump ring. Attach the jump ring to one end of a 15" chain length. Use a jump ring to attach the other end of the chain to the remaining silver oval.

3. For the yellow beaded strand, use a crimp bead to attach an 18" wire length to a jump ring. Thread the yellow and white beads on the wire until the beaded section is 14" long. Use a crimp bead to attach the wire to a jump ring.

4. For the clear beaded strand, use a crimp bead to attach a 19" wire length to a jump ring. Thread the clear beads on the wire until the beaded section is $14^1/_2$" long. Use a crimp bead to attach the wire to a jump ring.

5. For the blue beaded strand, use a crimp bead to attach a 21" wire length to a jump ring. Thread the blue beads on wire until the beaded section is 16" long. Use a crimp bead to attach the wire to a jump ring.

6. Attach the jump rings on the three beaded strands to the silver ovals on the daisy strand.

MEDALLION BRACELET

You'll need:

◆ silver/turquoise medallion
◆ large stone beads (we used 4)
◆ small irregularly-shaped stone beads (we used 12)
◆ silver toggle clasp
◆ silver nylon-coated beading wire
◆ silver crimp beads and crimp tool
◆ chain-nose pliers and wire cutters
◆ spring bead stops

Read Jewelry Making Basics, pages 90-96, before making your bracelet.

To make the bracelet:

1. Cut two 12" lengths of wire. Use crimp beads *(page 96)* to attach the middle of each wire to the medallion on opposite sides *(Fig. 1)*. Holding the ends of one wire together, thread the beads on the wire, using the spring bead stop to temporarily secure the beads. Repeat to thread the beads on the opposite wire. Check the bracelet size, adding or removing beads until the bracelet is the right length.

Fig. 1

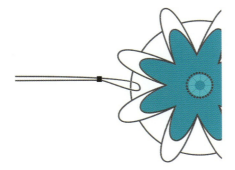

2. Use crimp beads to attach the wire ends to jump rings. Attach the clasp to the bracelet *(page 95)*.

DAISY EARRINGS

You'll need:
◆ 2 blue acrylic daisy beads
◆ 2 gold beads for daisy centers
◆ 2 blue seed beads
◆ 2 large silver kidney ear wires
◆ 2 silver jump rings
◆ silver nylon-coated beading wire
◆ silver crimp beads and crimp tool
◆ wire cutters

Read Jewelry Making Basics, pages 90-96, before making your earrings.

For each earring:
1. Thread the seed bead on an 8" wire length and fold the wire in half. Thread the wire ends through the beads, a crimp bead, and a jump ring *(Fig. 1)*. Thread the wire ends back through the crimp bead and the daisy bead. Secure the crimp bead *(page 96)* and trim the excess wire.

Fig. 1

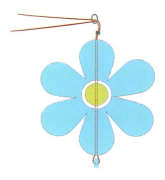

2. Slide the jump ring on an ear wire.

GREEN DANGLES NECKLACE

Approx. length: 25", excluding pendant

You'll need:

- assorted large, medium, and small green and silver beads
- assorted silver charms
- large silver decorative ring
- small silver link chain
- silver ball chain with ball closure
- silver eye pin
- silver head pins
- silver jump rings
- chain-nose pliers, round-nose pliers, and wire cutters

Read Jewelry Making Basics, pages 90-96, before making your necklace.

To make the necklace:

1. To make the beaded connector, thread a long bead on an eye pin. Make a loop *(page 95)* at the wire end *(Photo 1)*.

Photo 1

2. Make 4 bead dangles using the head pins and 1-7 beads per dangle. Use a jump ring *(page 95)* to attach a dangle to the beaded connector.
3. Make 6 chain dangles using the link chain, charms, bead dangles, and jump rings, varying the chain lengths from ⁵/₈"-1".
4. Use the jump rings to attach the beaded connector, bead dangles, and chain dangles to the silver ring.
5. Use a jump ring to attach a 25" length of ball chain to the silver ring.

CHAPTER FOUR

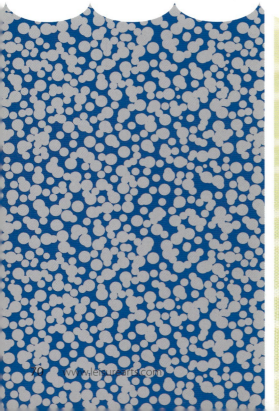

charmed

You can wear gorgeous charm beads similar to those sold in jewelry stores—at a fraction of the cost! The stunning metal-lined glass beads combine beautifully with accents and pendants to create these fresh new looks. All the easy basics on beads, findings, tools, and techniques begin on page 90. So have fun enriching your wardrobe with stylish jewelry for every outfit and occasion!

BANGLE BRACELET

You'll need:
- ◆ silver bangle bracelet with removable ends
- ◆ 6 assorted blue/green/white metal-lined glass beads
- ◆ 3 pink jeweled spacer beads
- ◆ 3 assorted silver spacer beads with attached charms

Read Jewelry Making Basics, pages 90-96, before making your bracelet.

To make the bracelet:
1. Remove 1 bracelet end.
2. Thread the beads and spacers on the bracelet.
3. Replace the bracelet end.

HEART NECKLACE

You'll need:
◆ silver pre-made necklace
◆ silver open heart pendant for metal-lined glass beads
◆ zebra stripe metal-lined glass bead
◆ amber jeweled spacer bead
◆ silver spacer bead with attached loop
◆ assorted small beads and a faux pearl charm
◆ silver head pins
◆ silver jump rings
◆ chain-nose pliers, round-nose pliers, and wire cutters

Read Jewelry Making Basics, pages 90-96, before making your necklace.

To make the necklace:
1. Make 3 bead dangles *(page 95)* using the head pins and assorted beads.
2. Attach each dangle to a jump ring *(page 95)*.
3. Attach the charm and dangles to another jump ring. Attach the jump ring to the spacer loop.
4. Unscrew the end from the heart pendant. Thread the beads and spacers on the pendant. Replace the end.
5. Thread the pendant on the necklace.

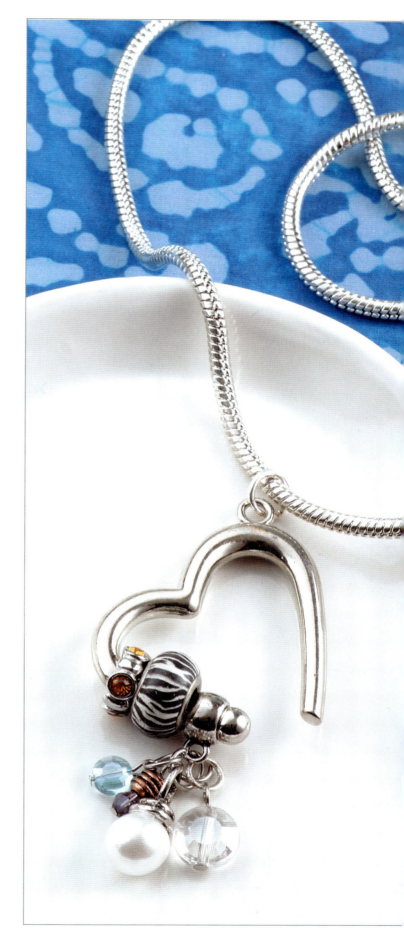

RIBBON BRACELET
& STRETCHY BRACELETS

For the ribbon bracelet, you'll need:
◆ 5 assorted metal-lined glass beads
◆ 6 assorted jeweled spacer beads
◆ 4 assorted silver spacer beads
◆ 3/8" wide ribbon

For each stretchy bracelet, you'll need:
◆ assorted beads and spacers (about 33-42)
◆ stretch cord
◆ jeweler's glue
◆ flexible wire beading needle

Read Jewelry Making Basics, pages 90-96, before making your bracelets.

To make the ribbon bracelet:
1. Thread the beads and spacers on a 20" length of ribbon.
2. Check the bracelet size, tie the ribbon into a bow, and trim the ends.

To make each stretchy bracelet:
1. With a bead stop at one end, thread the beads (and spacers) on a 12" length of cord *(Fig. 1)*.

Fig. 1

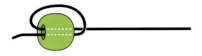

2. Check the bracelet size, adding or removing beads/spacers until the bracelet is the right length. Remove the bead stop. Tie the cord with a surgeon's knot *(Fig. 2)* and apply a drop of glue to the knot. Once dry, trim the cord ends.

Fig. 2

BOW BRACELET

You'll need:

◆ 18" leather cord necklace
◆ 6 assorted pink/black metal-lined beads
◆ 3 pink jeweled spacer beads
◆ ⅛" wide pink ribbon

Read Jewelry Making Basics, pages 90-96, before making your bracelet.

To make the bracelet:

1. Thread the beads on the necklace.
2. Loop the necklace to make a doubled bracelet.
3. To hold the loops in place, tie the cords together with 2 ribbon bows.

DANGLE EARRINGS

You'll need:

- ◆ 2 purple metal-lined beads
- ◆ 2 pink crystal metal-lined beads
- ◆ 2 medium crystal beads
- ◆ 2 silver/rhinestone spacers
- ◆ 2 small faux pearl beads
- ◆ 4 silver flat beads
- ◆ 2 silver head pins
- ◆ 2 silver ear wires with attached rhinestones
- ◆ chain-nose pliers, round-nose pliers, and wire cutters

Read Jewelry Making Basics, pages 90-96, before making your earrings.

For each earring:

1. Make a bead dangle *(page 95)* with the beads, a spacer, and a headpin.
2. Slide the dangle on the ear wire.

ELEPHANT CHOKER

You'll need:

- ◆ silver wire choker with removable magnetic clasp
- ◆ elephant pendant with attached bail
- ◆ 2 metal spacer beads
- ◆ 4 metal spacer beads with attached loops
- ◆ 6 assorted jeweled spacer beads
- ◆ 2 crystal charms
- ◆ 5 assorted charms
- ◆ 7 assorted small beads
- ◆ silver head pins
- ◆ silver jump rings
- ◆ chain-nose pliers, round-nose pliers, and wire cutters

Read Jewelry Making Basics, pages 90-96, before making your choker.

To make the choker:

1. Make 6 bead dangles *(page 95)* using the head pins and 1-2 assorted beads.
2. Use the jump rings *(page 95)* to attach the bead dangles and assorted charms to the spacer bead loops.
3. Unscrew one end of the clasp.
4. Thread the spacer beads, crystal charms, and pendant on the choker.
5. Replace the clasp end.

AMBER PENDANT NECKLACE

You'll need:
◆ velvet cord 18" necklace
◆ large amber acrylic gemstone
◆ 6 white/brown metal-lined glass beads
◆ 4 amber jeweled spacer beads
◆ assorted small beads and silver/rhinestone spacers for pendant
◆ silver bail
◆ silver nylon-coated beading wire
◆ silver crimp bead and crimp tool
◆ wire cutters

Read Jewelry Making Basics, pages 90-96, before making your necklace.

To make the necklace:
1. For the pendant, thread a 12" wire length through a small bead. With the bead centered on the wire, fold the wire in half and thread the small beads, spacers, and gemstone on the wire *(Fig. 1)*. Use a crimp bead *(page 96)* to attach the wire ends to the bail *(Fig. 2)*.

Fig. 1

Fig. 2

2. Thread the remaining beads, spacers, and pendant on the necklace.

FILIGREE CROSS NECKLACE

Approx. length: 31", excluding pendant

You'll need:
◆ metal filigree cross pendant with attached bail and pearl dangles **(Photo 1)**
◆ silver chain
◆ 6 aqua and green metal-lined glass beads
◆ 4 aqua and green jeweled spacer beads
◆ 6 silver metal spacer beads
◆ 2 large silver jump rings
◆ silver toggle clasp
◆ chain-nose pliers and wire cutters

Photo 1

Read Jewelry Making Basics, pages 90-96, before making your necklace.

To make the necklace:
1. Thread the beads, spacers, and pendant on a 30" chain length.
2. Use the jump rings *(page 95)* to attach the clasp to the chain.

PURPLE RIBBON BRACELET

You'll need:

◆ 5 assorted purple metal-lined glass beads
◆ 3 assorted purple jeweled spacer beads
◆ purple ⅛" wide ribbon, ¼" wide ribbon, and cord (12" each)
◆ 2 silver jump rings
◆ 2 silver cord ends
◆ silver lobster clasp
◆ chain-nose pliers

Read Jewelry Making Basics, pages 90-96, before making your bracelet.

To make the bracelet:

1. Holding the ribbons and cord together, use the chain-nose pliers to attach a cord end. Use a jump ring *(page 95)* to attach the clasp to the cord end.
2. Thread the beads and spacers on the cord/ribbon.
3. Check the bracelet size. Trim the cord/ribbon to the determined length. Holding the ends together, attach the remaining cord end and jump ring.

CROSS NECKLACE

Approx. length: 28", excluding pendant

You'll need:
◆ metal cross pendant with attached chains and bail
◆ 8 red/black/silver metal-lined glass beads
◆ 5 red/black jeweled spacer beads
◆ 3 silver spacer beads, 1 with attached loop
◆ 4 assorted medium and small red, black, and silver beads
◆ black heart charm
◆ 2 silver cones
◆ 1¹/₈ yds sheer red ribbon
◆ small black chain
◆ black cord
◆ silver toggle clasp
◆ silver eye pins
◆ silver head pins
◆ silver jump rings
◆ silver large oval jump ring
◆ chain-nose pliers, round-nose pliers, and wire cutters

Read Jewelry Making Basics, pages 90-96, before making your necklace.

To make the necklace:
1. Make a bead dangle *(page 95)* with a black bead and head pin.
2. Attach the charm to the spacer loop with a jump ring *(page 95)*.
3. To make the beaded connector, thread the remaining assorted beads, a jeweled spacer, and the charm spacer on an eye pin. Make a loop at the wire end *(Photo 1)*.

Photo 1

4. Attach the bead dangle to the connector. Attach the connector to the cross with the large oval jump ring.
5. Cut a 28" length each of ribbon, cord, and chain.
6. Attach an eye pin to the chain about ¹/₂" from one end. Holding ends together, tightly wrap the eye pin around the ribbon, cord, and chain *(Fig. 1)*.

Fig. 1

7. Thread the eye pin end through a cone and pull until the wrapped ends are drawn into the cone *(Fig. 2)*. Attach the eye pin to one end of the clasp.

Fig. 2

8. Thread the beads, spacers, and pendant on the necklace.
9. Repeat Steps 6 and 7 to attach the remaining cone and clasp end to the necklace.
10. Knot 6" ribbon lengths between the beads.

HOOP EARRINGS

You'll need:

◆ 2 silver hoop earrings
◆ 2 teal metal-lined glass beads
◆ 4 silver spacers

Read Jewelry Making Basics, pages 90-96, before making your earrings.

For each earring:

Thread 1 bead and 2 spacers on a hoop.

TIP: *Just about everyone has a pair of hoop earrings in her jewelry box. This is a great way to accessorize them.*

LINKED BEADS NECKLACE

Approx. length: 36"

You'll need:
◆ faux pearl linked beads chain
◆ 5 purple and clear metal-lined beads
◆ 2 purple jeweled spacer beads
◆ 2 silver spacer beads
◆ chain-nose pliers and wire cutters

Read Jewelry Making Basics, pages 90-96, before making your necklace.

To make the necklace:
1. Thread the beads and spacers on a 36" chain length.
2. Join the links between the pearls to complete the necklace *(page 95)*.

KEY NECKLACE

Approx. length: 30", excluding pendant

You'll need:

◆ key pendant for large metal-lined glass beads
◆ 2 blue metal-lined glass beads
◆ 2 blue and crystal jeweled spacer beads
◆ silver chain
◆ 3 decorative silver circle links
◆ assorted medium and small blue beads (we used 34)
◆ assorted medium and small silver beads (we used 26)
◆ silver nylon-coated beading wire
◆ large silver jump rings
◆ silver crimp beads and crimp tool
◆ chain-nose pliers and wire cutters

Read Jewelry Making Basics, pages 90-96, before making your necklace.

To make the necklace:

1. Unscrew the top of the key pendant. Thread the metal-lined beads and jeweled spacer beads on the pendant and replace the top. Attach the pendant to a decorative circle link with a jump ring *(page 95)*.
2. Attach a decorative circle link to each end of an 18" chain length.

3. Use a crimp bead *(page 96)* to attach a 12" wire length to one link on the chain *(Fig. 1)*. Thread blue and silver beads on the wire until the beaded section is 6" long.

Fig. 1

4. Use a crimp bead to attach the pendant link *(Fig. 2)*.

Fig. 2

5. Repeat Steps 3-4 to complete the necklace.

OWL BRACELET

You'll need:

◆ silver bracelet for metal-lined beads
◆ owl pendant
◆ 6 blue metal lined beads
◆ 5 blue/crystal jeweled spacer beads
◆ 9 assorted silver spacer beads
◆ ¹⁄₄" wide silver ribbon
◆ jeweler's glue

Read Jewelry Making Basics, pages 90-96, before making your bracelet.

To make the bracelet:

1. Thread the pendant, a blue jeweled spacer, and a silver spacer on an 8" ribbon length.
2. Thread the remaining beads and spacers on the bracelet.
3. Tie the ribbon to the bracelet with a surgeon's knot *(Fig. 1)* and apply a drop of glue to the knot. Once dry, trim the ribbon ends.

Fig. 1

DANGLE NECKLACE

You'll need:

◆ pre-made leather cord necklace
◆ pre-made beaded cluster **(Photo 1)**
◆ 6 assorted silver metal spacer beads
◆ 3 black and crystal jeweled spacer beads
◆ chain-nose pliers

Photo 1

Read Jewelry Making Basics, pages 90-96, before making your necklace.

To make the necklace:

1. For the pendant, use the jump ring *(page 95)* to attach the beaded cluster to a jeweled spacer bead.
2. Thread the beads, spacers, and pendant on the necklace.

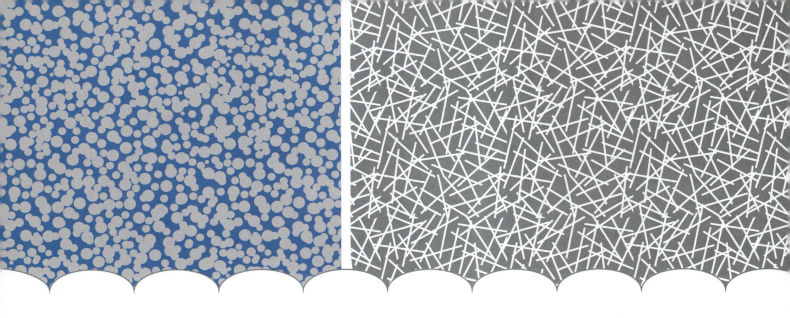

JEWELRY MAKING BASICS

Sizing It Up

This table and drawing show various necklace lengths and about where they fall on the body. The lengths are commonly used in the jewelry world, but feel free to adjust your necklaces to suit you and your fashion sense.

Common Jewelry Lengths

Bracelet	6" to 8"
Choker	14" to 16"
Princess	17" to 19"
Matinee	20" to 24"
Opera	28" to 34"
Rope	40" to 45"
Lariat	Over 45"

CHOOSING BEADS

Beads come in all sizes, shapes, colors, finishes, and materials.

Ceramic and stone beads come in several shapes and may be glazed or similarly textured.

Plastic or acrylic beads are lightweight and can give a more whimsical look to your jewelry. Some metal-look beads are plastic; others may be highly polished to look like glass.

Crystal beads have multiple machine-cut facets that capture and reflect light with lots of sparkle. They come in dozens of colors, sizes, and shapes.

Seed beads are usually the smallest beads and are available in different sizes, shapes, and colors. This category includes small round beads, small tube beads, bugle beads, and the larger e-beads.

Faux pearls have a synthetic coating over a crystal, glass, or plastic base. They are very uniform in size, shape, and color.

Shell beads have a lustrous finish. They can be uniform in size, shape, and color or be more varied and organic. They can even be actual whole shells!

Glass beads come in all sizes, shapes, and colors. Some have a shiny, polished, or iridescent finish, while others may have a matte finish.

Wood beads give your jewelry a natural, organic look. They are available in many sizes, shapes, and finishes.

Metal beads, including spacers and spacer beads, can be made of base metal (which is non-precious) or plated metals.

CHOOSING FINDINGS

Findings are the components used to assemble jewelry.

Beading thread is strong and has very little stretch. This soft thread easily passes through a beading needle's eye, knots well, and will create a soft, flowing jewelry piece.

Chains come in a variety of sizes, styles, colors, and finishes.

Leather and suede cords come in a variety of sizes and colors and are used for a more casual look.

Nylon-coated beading wire is made up of multiple strands of metal that are twisted together and coated with nylon; the more strands, the stronger and more flexible the wire. It is available in various diameters and strengths.

Stretch cord is great for bracelets and is more durable than thin elastic. A drop of jeweler's glue on the knot will keep the bracelet secure.

Cord is available in many colors and may be cotton, linen, or jute.

Bead caps add texture and sparkle when placed next to beads.

Clasps of all sizes, shapes, and styles are available. Lobster clasps are shaped like a lobster's claw and have a spring-action closure. A toggle clasp is secured by sliding the bar through the loop. There are also spring-ring clasps, hook and eye clasps, box clasps, and magnetic clasps.

Cones are findings that hide the ends of multi-strand jewelry pieces.

Cord ends fit over the ends of ribbon, leather, and cord. They may be crimped and/or glued in place.

Crimp beads or tubes are small metal beads that are flattened over jewelry wire to finish the ends or hold elements in place. The beads are rounded and the tubes are cylinder-shaped. Both come in many sizes and finishes.

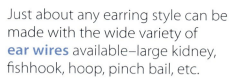

Just about any earring style can be made with the wide variety of **ear wires** available–large kidney, fishhook, hoop, pinch bail, etc.

Head pins & eye pins are very similar and are used in similar situations when making jewelry. A head pin is a straight wire with a head of some sort; many are flat, but there are several decorative styles as well. An eye pin is also a straight wire, but it has a loop at one end. This loop may be opened and closed with chain-nose pliers, just like a jump ring.

Jump rings are metal rounds or ovals that are used to attach jewelry components to each other. The rings are opened and closed with chain-nose pliers.

Spacer bars keep beaded strands separate on bracelets and necklaces. Some are very decorative and become a design element, while others are more discreet in their appearance.

TOOLS & HOW TO USE THEM

The two most common types of **beading needles** are the flexible wire needle and the rigid metal needle. The eye of the flexible wire needle collapses on itself, making it easier to go through small-hole beads.

Bead mats are made of foam-like material and keep the beads from rolling all over the work surface.

Bead boards are very handy. Not only can you see your necklace or bracelet in its final arrangement, the board also has measurements so that you no longer have to guess how many beads you'll need for a specific length.

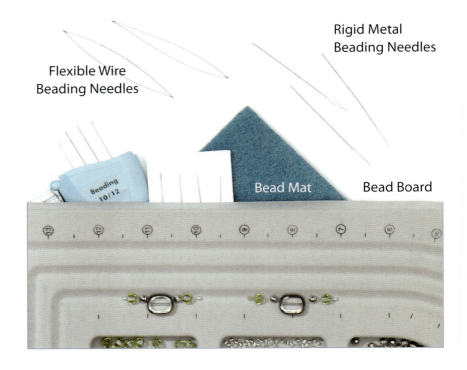

Flexible Wire Beading Needles

Rigid Metal Beading Needles

Bead Mat

Bead Board

Chain-nose pliers have rounded, tapered jaws and a flat interior surface that will not mar wire or metal findings. These pliers are used for opening and closing jump rings and bending wire. They may also be called needle-nose pliers. You'll need 2 pair to open jump rings and loops on head pins and eye pins.

Round-nose pliers have round jaws that are useful for making loops and bending wire smoothly.

Wire cutters are used to cut beading wire, head pins, eye pins, and other soft metals.

A **crimp tool** (also known as crimping pliers) flattens and shapes the crimp bead or crimp tube.

Spring bead stops keep beads from sliding off when threading beads on beading wire. Just squeeze the ends and slip the wire between the spring coils.

Spring bead stops

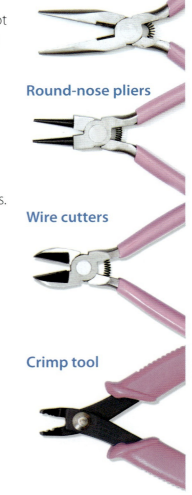

Chain-nose pliers

Round-nose pliers

Wire cutters

Crimp tool

BASIC TECHNIQUES

Using a Bead Stop

When threading beads on a thread or cord, you don't want to be concerned that the beads will slide off the other end. A bead stop does just that: it stops the beads from sliding off your beading thread.

You can simply use a larger, different colored bead. Before you start threading on your beads, thread on a bead stop. Run the beading thread or cord around the bead and pass through the bead again, securing it in place **(Fig. 1)**.

Fig. 1

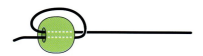

When you are ready to knot the ends, loosen the thread or cord and carefully remove the bead stop. You can now tie a surgeon's knot *(page 96)*.

Making Bead Dangles on Head Pins

Slide your beads on a head pin. Leaving about ¹/₂", cut off the excess wire. If you are making a large loop, leave more wire at the end.

Using the chain-nose pliers, bend the wire at a 90° angle **(Fig. 2)**. Grasp the wire end with the round-nose pliers. Turn the pliers and bend the wire into a loop **(Figs. 3-4)**. Release the pliers. Straighten or twist the loop further if necessary.

Loops may also be made on eye pins the same way.

Fig. 2

Fig. 3

Fig. 4

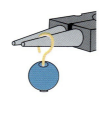

Opening and Closing Jump Rings and Loops on Head Pins or Eye Pins

Whether you need to attach a clasp, charm, dangle, or other jewelry component, you'll probably use jump rings. Here's how to properly open and close them.

Pick up a jump ring with chain-nose pliers. With a second pair of chain-nose pliers, gently hold the other side of the ring. Open the ring by pulling one pair of pliers toward you while pushing the other away **(Fig. 5)**.

Fig. 5

Close the ring by pushing and pulling the pliers in the opposite direction, bringing the ring ends back together.

You'll also open and close the loops on head pins and eye pins the same way.

Using Crimp Beads Or Tubes

To finish a wire end, thread a crimp bead or tube and the clasp or jump ring on the wire. Run the wire back through the crimp bead; use a pair of pliers to pull and tighten the wire *(Fig. 6)*. Place the crimp bead or tube on the inner groove of the crimp tool and squeeze *(Fig. 7)*.

Release the tool, turn the crimp bead or tube a quarter turn, and place it in the outer groove *(Fig. 8)*. Squeeze the tool to round out the crimp bead or tube *(Fig. 9)*. Trim the wire end or if the design calls for beads, thread the beads over the wire to cover the end.

Fig. 6

Fig. 7

Fig. 8

Fig. 9

Tying Knots

Tie an **overhand knot** with cords, suede cords, or ribbon *(Fig. 10)*.

Fig. 10

Tie a **surgeon's knot** *(Fig. 11)* when using stretch cord or beading thread. Add a drop of jeweler's glue to the knot for extra strength.

Fig. 11